GIANT VEHICLES
An Imagination Library Series

GIANT DIGGERS

Jim Mezzanotte

GARETH**STEVENS**

PUBLISHING

A Member of the WRC Media Family of Companies

Please visit our web site at: www.garethstevens.com
For a free color catalog describing Gareth Stevens Publishing's list of high-quality books
and multimedia programs, call 1-800-542-2595 (USA) or 1-800-387-3178 (Canada).
Gareth Stevens Publishing's fax: (414) 332-3567.

Library of Congress Cataloging-in-Publication Data

Mezzanotte, Jim.
    Giant diggers / by Jim Mezzanotte.
       p. cm. — (Giant vehicles)
    Includes bibliographical references and index.
    ISBN 0-8368-4911-6 (lib. bdg.)
    ISBN 0-8368-4918-3 (softcover)
    1. Excavating machinery—Juvenile literature. I. Title.
  TA735.M64   2005
  621.8'65—dc22   2005045153

First published in 2006 by
Gareth Stevens Publishing
A Member of the WRC Media Family of Companies
330 West Olive Street, Suite 100
Milwaukee, WI 53212 USA

Editorial direction: Mark J. Sachner
Editor: JoAnn Early Macken
Art direction: Tammy West
Cover design and page layout: Kami M. Koenig
Photo editor: Diane Laska-Swanke
Picture researcher: Martin Levick

Photo credits: Cover, pp. 5, 9, 15, 17 © Eric Orlemann; pp. 7, 19, 21 Courtesy of Bucyrus International, Inc.;
pp. 11, 13 © Keith Haddock

Printed in the United States of America

1 2 3 4 5 6 7 8 9 09 08 07 06 05

COVER: The Bucyrus company
made this giant digger. It
looks like a big factory!

Table of Contents

Words that appear in the glossary are printed in **boldface** type the first time they occur in the text.

Giants on Land

Giant diggers are huge machines. The biggest ones are taller than most buildings. On land, they are the largest **mobile** machines in the world. Only giant ships are larger. A digger is also called an excavator.

Most giant diggers work in **mines**. They work in surface mines. These mines are big holes. The diggers make the holes. They move huge amounts of earth.

There are different kinds of giant diggers in different sizes. But they are all big. They are too big to travel in one piece. They travel to mines in parts. At the mines, they are put together. Putting together one giant digger can take years!

*This giant digger is working in a **coal** mine. It digs up earth to reach the coal. Workers put it together at the mine site.*

Bigger and Better

The first diggers were built in the 1800s. They moved on rails like trains. They were much smaller than today's diggers.

Diggers kept improving. They got bigger. Their top parts turned in a circle so they could dig and unload and stay in one place. They used **tracks**. Tracks are belts. The belts turn on a row of wheels. With tracks, diggers could go anywhere.

By the 1920s, companies were building huge diggers. But the diggers kept growing. By the 1960s, companies were making the biggest diggers ever built.

The Bucyrus company made this early digger. It moved on rails and used steam power just like the train behind it.

Giant Shovels

A mining shovel is one kind of giant digger. It has a big bucket with teeth. This bucket is called a dipper. It scoops up dirt. **Cables** are attached to the dipper. The cables pull up on the dipper to make it dig. The dipper is big — you could park a few cars inside!

Stripping shovels are the largest mining shovels. They dig long strips of earth. They have a long reach. The shovels can dump earth far from where they dig it. Some of the largest diggers in the world have been stripping shovels.

This dipper is big. But some dippers are even bigger! You can see the dipper's teeth on the bottom edge. They cut into the earth.

Digging With Draglines

A dragline is like a giant **crane**. Instead of using a hook for lifting, it has a bucket. The bucket hangs from cables. It is lowered to the ground. Other cables, or lines, drag it toward the machine. The bucket scoops up the dirt.

Draglines are huge machines. Their buckets can be as big as houses! Like stripping shovels, they dig holes for mines. They cost millions of dollars.

A dragline does not roll on tracks. Instead, it "walks." It has long metal boxes called shoes on each side. They push it up and then back. It always moves back, away from the hole.

The P&H company makes this dragline. After the bucket unloads, it drops to the ground. The draglines pull it, and it scoops more earth.

Smaller—But Still Huge!

Some giant diggers do not use cables. They use **hydraulic** cylinders. A cylinder is a big tube. Inside, it has a smaller tube called a piston. Oil goes into the cylinder. The oil pushes the piston, and it slides out. These diggers have many cylinders. The cylinders lift and lower the bucket to scoop earth.

These diggers are smaller than other giant diggers. But they are still huge! They can weigh more than one million pounds. They are as tall as three-story buildings. These diggers work fast. They can load a giant dump truck in minutes.

Komatsu makes this digger. It is called a hydraulic excavator. You can see its many hydraulic cylinders. Its bucket drops huge loads of earth into the dump truck.

Digger Power

Diggers need powerful engines. Some diggers have big **diesel** engines. The engines use diesel **fuel**, not gasoline. These engines are much larger than car engines. A digger often has two engines. Together, they can produce twenty times more **horsepower** than car engines.

Larger diggers use electric motors. They need a long cord, just like a vacuum cleaner! The cord is very thick. It is wrapped around a big drum. As the digger moves, more cord rolls out. The diggers use many motors. Some motors lift the bucket. Other motors make the digger move. A giant digger can use as much electricity as a small town!

This giant digger has electric motors. You can see its cord and drum. The cord gives it electricity. As it moves, the cord rolls off the drum.

How Big is Big?

The Marion company built the largest shovel in the world. It was called the Captain. It was built in 1965. The Captain was a stripping shovel. Only one was built. It cost fifteen million dollars! The Captain worked at a coal mine. It worked until 1991.

The Captain was one of the heaviest machines that ever moved on land. It weighed over 20 million pounds (9 million kilograms) — more than 5,000 cars! It was twenty-one stories high. The Captain's tracks were more than twice the height of an adult. Its dipper could easily hold six cars. The Captain was one big machine!

This huge digger is the Marion 6360. People called it the Captain. It was one of the biggest land vehicles ever built. Can you spot the person operating it?

Digger Jobs

At mines, valuable things are taken from the ground. They include coal, gold, and silver. To reach them, giant diggers remove layers of earth. Later, the diggers put the earth back. The diggers work every day, all year. They work at night, too. Most giant diggers work at one mine. They may work there for more than thirty years.

For some jobs, a huge dragline is best. It moves big loads a long distance, so trucks are not needed. For other jobs, a smaller digger is best. It loads earth into trucks. The trucks take away the earth. The digger loads one truck after another. It never stops working!

"Big Muskie" was the largest dragline ever built. It worked at this mine for more than twenty years. It makes the other giant diggers seem tiny!

Let's Dig!

A digger's cab is high in the air. You climb stairs to get up to it. There are large windows so you can see all around. The cab is quiet and **spacious**. It keeps you comfortable while you work. A separate room has a microwave oven and a refrigerator.

Operating a giant digger takes skill. You have to move the big bucket to dig. You have to swing it around to unload. You have to move the machine, too. Computer screens tell you if something is wrong. The digger moves huge loads of earth, so you have to be careful. Its power is at your command!

This man is operating a dragline at a mine. He has to control that huge bucket. It is far below him! You can see the two lines that drag the bucket.

More to Read and View

Books

C is for Construction: Big Trucks and Diggers from A to Z. Caterpillar (Chronicle Books)

Digger. Machines at Work (series) Nicola Deschamps (DK Publishing)

Diggers. Heavy Equipment (series). David Armentrout and Patricia Armentrout (Rourke Publishing)

Earth Movers. Mighty Movers (series). Sarah Tieck (Buddy Books)

Monster Road Builders. Angela Royston (Barron's)

Road Builders. B. G. Hennessy (Viking)

DVDs and Videos

Earth Movers (A&E Entertainment)

Great Big Diggers and Dozers (Library Video)

Heavy Equipment Operator: Dump Trucks, Dirt Movers, and More. What Do You Want to Be When You Grow Up (series) (Tapeworm)

I Dig Dirt (Big Kids Productions)

I Love Big Machines (Consumervision)

Web Sites

Web sites change frequently, but we believe the following web sites are going to last. You can also use good search engines, such as **Yahooligans!** (www.yahooligans.com) or **Google** (www.google.com) to find more information about giant vehicles. Some keywords that will help you are *Bucyrus, draglines, electric shovels, excavators, P&H, stripping shovels,* and *Terex.*

auto.howstuffworks.com/
  diesel1.htm
This web site shows how a diesel engine works.

members.tripod.com/
  dsmdonaldson/id59.htm
At this web site, you can see pictures of early steam shovels.

science.howstuffworks.com/
  hydraulic.htm
Visit this web site to learn more about how hydraulic machines work.

www.bucyrus.com/draglines.htm
At this web site, you can see pictures of huge draglines made by the Bucyrus company.

www.kenkenkikki.jp/special/no01/
  e_index.htm
At this site, you can learn how a hydraulic digger works.

www.liebherr.com/me/en/47592.asp
This web site has pictures of many different hydraulic diggers. They are made by the Liebherr company.

www.phmining.com/photos/
  index.html
Visit this web site to see a photo gallery of diggers made by the P&H company.

www.stripmine.org/stripmnu.htm
Visit this site to see many pictures of huge draglines and stripping shovels, including the "Captain."

Glossary

You can find these words on the pages listed. Reading a word in a sentence helps you to understand it even better.

cables (KAY-bulz): thick metal ropes made from strands of wire that are twisted together. 8, 10, 12

coal (KOLE): a black material made of long-dead plants. Coal is a fuel, and it is often used to power electric power plants. 4, 16, 18

crane (KRAYN): a machine that lifts and moves things. A crane has a tall arm called a boom. A cable hangs down from this boom. It slides on pulleys to lift things. 10

diesel (DEE-zull): the name for a kind of engine and the special fuel it uses. Most diesel engines are very reliable. They often use less fuel than gas engines. 14

fuel (FYULE): something that burns to provide energy. 14

horsepower (HORS-pow-ur): the amount of power an engine makes, based on how much work one horse can do. 14

hydraulic (hi-DRAW-lick): having to do with using water or another liquid to move something. 12

mines (MINES): places where coal, gold, silver, and other things are taken out of the ground. Some mines are underground tunnels. Other mines are big holes, or pits. 4, 10, 16, 18

mobile (MOE-bul): able to move around. 4

spacious (SPAY-shus): having a lot of room. 20

tracks (TRAX): belts that circle around a row of wheels to move a machine. One wheel in each belt makes it turn. Some tracks are metal plates linked together. Other tracks are loops made of rubber. 6, 16

Index